Jr. Graphic Mythologies™

MESOAMERICAN MYTHOLOGY

Quetzalcoatl

Tom Daning

PowerKiDS press.

New York

Published in 2007 by The Rosen Publishing Group, Inc.
29 East 21st Street, New York, NY 10010

Copyright © 2007 by The Rosen Publishing Group, Inc.

First Edition
Editor: Julia Wong
Book Design: Greg Tucker
Illustrations: Q2A

Library of Congress Cataloging-in-Publication Data

Daning, Tom.
  Mesoamerican mythology : Quetzalcoatl / by Tom Daning.— 1st ed.
      p. cm. — (Jr. graphic mythologies)
  Includes index.
  ISBN (10) 1-4042-3401-2 (13) 978-1-4042-3401-7 (lib. bdg.) —
ISBN (10) 1-4042-2154-9 (13) 978-1-4042-2154-3 (pbk.)
  1. Quetzalcoatl (Aztec deity)—Juvenile literature. 2. Aztec mythology—Juvenile
literature. I. Title. II. Series.
  F1219.76.R45D36 2007
  299'.78452—dc22
                                        2006003371

Manufactured in the United States of America

CONTENTS

MAJOR CHARACTERS

Quetzalcoatl *(keht-sahl-KOH-atl) was one of the gods who helped create the world. He worked to make the gods and people work together in peace. He could become a snake that was covered in feathers.*

Tezcatlipoca *(tehs-kah-tlee-POH-kah) was often an enemy of Quetzalcoatl. He was the god of the night and of fighting. He carried a magical mirror and could become a large wild cat.*

Tlatecuhtli *(tlah-teh-KOO-tlee) was the monster goddess of the sea. She was part alligator and part snake. She ate all the animals that lived in the sea.*

QUETZALCOATL

LONG AGO, THE MESOAMERICAN GODS LIVED IN A **PARADISE** CALLED TALOCAN.

TALOCAN'S MOST **BELOVED** AND POWERFUL GOD WAS QUETZALCOATL.

QUETZALCOATL WAS RESPECTED BECAUSE HE BROUGHT **UNITY** TO THE GODS.

QUETZALCOATL WAS ALSO CALLED THE FEATHERED **SERPENT**.

ALSO IN TALOCAN THERE LIVED A GOD NAMED TEZCATLIPOCA.

TEZCATLIPOCA WAS ALSO VERY POWERFUL.

WHEREVER HE WENT, TEZCATLIPOCA BROUGHT **DISCORD**, FIGHTING, AND WAR. HE OFTEN **DISGUISED** HIMSELF AS A **JAGUAR**.

ONE DAY QUETZALCOATL WAS LOOKING DOWN FROM TALOCAN TO THE SEA BELOW. HE WAS **HORRIFIED** BY WHAT HE SAW.

NO! NOT AGAIN!

IN THE WATER WAS THE GREAT **CAIMAN**, TLATECUHTLI.

THE GODDESS TLATECUHTLI RULED THE SEA. SHE ATE WHATEVER SHE FOUND.

QUETZALCOATL HAD CREATED FISH, SEALS, AND SEA TURTLES TO LIVE IN THE SEA.

WHATEVER CREATURES QUETZALCOATL CREATED, TLATECUHTLI DESTROYED.

TEZCATLIPOCA MADE CREATURES FOR THE SEA TOO. NO MATTER HOW MANY SHARKS OR GIANT SQUID HE MADE, TLATECUHTLI ATE THOSE TOO!

THE TWO GODS MET ONE DAY TO TALK ABOUT THE TROUBLE WITH TLATECUHTLI.

YOU AND I ARE VERY DIFFERENT, YET WE HAVE THE SAME ENEMY.

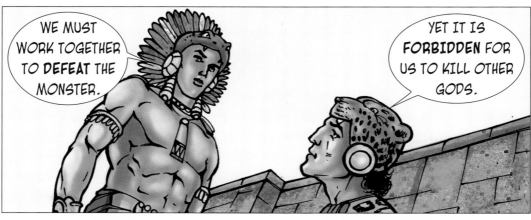

WE MUST WORK TOGETHER TO **DEFEAT** THE MONSTER.

YET IT IS **FORBIDDEN** FOR US TO KILL OTHER GODS.

I FEAR WE HAVE NO OTHER CHOICE.

QUETZALCOATL AND TEZCATLIPOCA DECIDED TO GO INTO THE SEA TO FIND TLATECUHTLI. THEY CHANGED INTO GIANT SERPENTS.

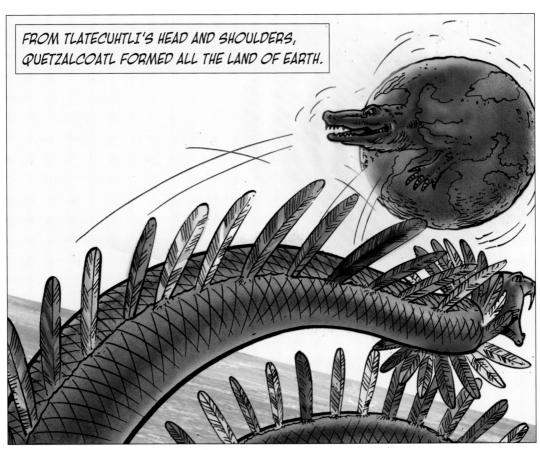

FROM TLATECUHTLI'S HEAD AND SHOULDERS, QUETZALCOATL FORMED ALL THE LAND OF EARTH.

FROM HER TAIL AND LEGS, TEZCATLIPOCA FORMED THE SKY.

THE GODS BEGAN TO DO THEIR OWN WORK UPON THE NEW LAND. FROM THE GREAT CAIMAN'S SCALES THEY CREATED TREES, GRASS, AND FLOWERS.

FROM HER EYES THEY CREATED CAVES, WATERFALLS, AND PONDS.

FROM THE CAIMAN'S MOUTH, THEY CREATED MIGHTY RIVERS.

FROM THE SHOULDERS OF TLATECUHTLI THE GODS MADE GREAT MOUNTAINS. FROM HER NOSE THEY MADE HILLS AND VALLEYS.

THE PEOPLE SAW WHAT THE GODS HAD DONE AND THEY GAVE THANKS.

THE END

FAMILY TREE

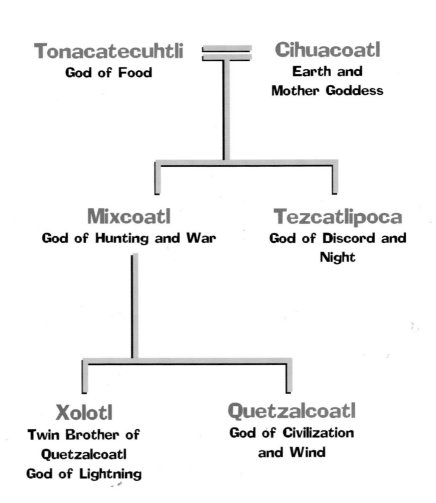

Tonacatecuhtli
God of Food

Cihuacoatl
Earth and
Mother Goddess

Mixcoatl
God of Hunting and War

Tezcatlipoca
God of Discord and
Night

Xolotl
Twin Brother of
Quetzalcoatl
God of Lightning

Quetzalcoatl
God of Civilization
and Wind

GLOSSARY

beloved (bih-LUVD) Dearly loved.

caiman (KAY-men) An alligator-like animal that lives in Central and South America.

defeat (dih-FEET) To win against someone in a game or battle.

discord (DIS-kawrd) Disagreement and fighting.

disguised (dis-GYZD) Wore a costume or an outfit to hide one's identity.

forbidden (fur-BIH-den) Not allowed.

horrified (HAWR-uh-fyd) Very upset and shocked.

jaguar (JA-gwahr) One of the four species of great cats. They live in Central and South America and have spotted coats.

paradise (PER-uh-dys) A wonderful, beautiful place.

punished (PUH-nisht) Caused someone pain or loss for a crime he or she has committed.

serpent (SUR-punt) A snake.

survive (sur-VYV) To stay alive.

unity (YOO-nuh-tee) Togetherness.

INDEX

WEB SITES

Due to the changing nature of Internet links, PowerKids Press has developed an online list of Web sites related to the subject of this book. This site is updated regularly. Please use this link to access the list:
www.powerkidslinks.com/myth/quetzal/